50 Rustic Italian Pizza Recipes for Home

By: Kelly Johnson

Table of Contents

- Margherita with Prosciutto Crudo
- Rustic Veggie Pizza
- Margherita with Fresh Mozzarella
- Rustic Italian Sausage and Peppers Pizza
- Margherita with Ricotta Cheese
- Rustic Italian Meat Lovers Pizza
- Margherita with Spinach and Ricotta
- Rustic Margherita with Fresh Tomatoes
- Margherita with Italian Ham
- Rustic Margherita with Pesto Drizzle
- Margherita with Gorgonzola Cheese
- Rustic Margherita with Arugula
- Margherita with Provolone Cheese
- Rustic Margherita with Pancetta
- Margherita with Grilled Vegetables

Margherita Pizza

Ingredients:

- 1 pizza dough (homemade or store-bought)
- 1/2 cup pizza sauce or crushed tomatoes
- 8 oz fresh mozzarella cheese, sliced
- Fresh basil leaves
- Extra-virgin olive oil
- Salt and pepper to taste
- Cornmeal or flour for dusting

Instructions:

1. Preheat your oven to the highest temperature it can go, typically around 500-550°F (260-290°C). If you have a pizza stone, place it in the oven to preheat as well.
2. Dust your work surface with cornmeal or flour to prevent sticking. Stretch or roll out the pizza dough into a circle, about 12 inches in diameter, or your desired thickness.
3. Transfer the stretched dough to a pizza peel or parchment paper dusted with cornmeal or flour.
4. Spread the pizza sauce evenly over the dough, leaving a small border around the edges.
5. Arrange the sliced mozzarella cheese evenly over the sauce.
6. Tear fresh basil leaves and scatter them over the cheese.
7. Drizzle a little extra-virgin olive oil over the pizza.
8. Season with salt and pepper to taste.
9. Carefully transfer the pizza to the preheated oven, either directly onto the pizza stone or onto a baking sheet if you're using parchment paper.
10. Bake the pizza for about 10-12 minutes, or until the crust is golden brown and the cheese is bubbly and melted.
11. Once done, remove the pizza from the oven and let it cool for a minute or two.
12. Slice the Margherita Pizza and serve hot. Optionally, you can garnish with additional fresh basil leaves and a drizzle of olive oil before serving.

Enjoy your homemade Margherita Pizza!

Pepperoni Pizza

Ingredients:

- 1 pizza dough (homemade or store-bought)
- 1/2 cup pizza sauce or marinara sauce
- 1 1/2 cups shredded mozzarella cheese
- 1/4 cup sliced pepperoni
- 1/4 cup sliced black olives (optional)
- 1/4 cup sliced mushrooms (optional)
- 1/4 teaspoon dried oregano
- 1/4 teaspoon dried basil
- Crushed red pepper flakes (optional)
- Olive oil (for drizzling)

Instructions:

1. Preheat your oven to the highest temperature it can go, typically around 500-550°F (260-290°C). If you have a pizza stone, place it in the oven to preheat as well.
2. Dust your work surface with cornmeal or flour to prevent sticking. Stretch or roll out the pizza dough into a circle, about 12 inches in diameter, or your desired thickness.
3. Transfer the stretched dough to a pizza peel or parchment paper dusted with cornmeal or flour.
4. Spread the pizza sauce evenly over the dough, leaving a small border around the edges.
5. Sprinkle the shredded mozzarella cheese evenly over the sauce.
6. Arrange the sliced pepperoni over the cheese. Add optional toppings like sliced black olives and mushrooms if desired.
7. Sprinkle dried oregano and dried basil over the pizza.
8. Drizzle a little olive oil over the pizza.
9. Optionally, sprinkle some crushed red pepper flakes for extra heat.
10. Carefully transfer the pizza to the preheated oven, either directly onto the pizza stone or onto a baking sheet if you're using parchment paper.
11. Bake the pizza for about 10-12 minutes, or until the crust is golden brown and the cheese is bubbly and melted.
12. Once done, remove the pizza from the oven and let it cool for a minute or two.
13. Slice the Pepperoni Pizza and serve hot.

Enjoy your homemade Pepperoni Pizza!

Neapolitan Pizza

Ingredients:

- 1 ball of Neapolitan pizza dough (homemade or store-bought)
- 1/2 cup San Marzano tomato sauce (strained or crushed)
- 4 oz fresh mozzarella cheese, sliced
- Fresh basil leaves
- Extra-virgin olive oil
- Salt to taste
- Semolina flour or cornmeal for dusting

Instructions:

1. Preheat your oven to the highest temperature it can go, typically around 500-550°F (260-290°C). If you have a pizza stone, place it in the oven to preheat as well.
2. Dust your work surface with semolina flour or cornmeal to prevent sticking. Gently stretch or roll out the pizza dough into a circle, about 10-12 inches in diameter. The crust should be thin, with slightly thicker edges.
3. Transfer the stretched dough to a pizza peel or parchment paper dusted with semolina flour or cornmeal.
4. Spread the San Marzano tomato sauce evenly over the dough, leaving a small border around the edges.
5. Arrange the sliced fresh mozzarella cheese evenly over the sauce.
6. Tear fresh basil leaves and scatter them over the cheese.
7. Drizzle a little extra-virgin olive oil over the pizza.
8. Sprinkle a pinch of salt over the pizza.
9. Carefully transfer the pizza to the preheated oven, either directly onto the pizza stone or onto a baking sheet if you're using parchment paper.
10. Bake the pizza for about 8-10 minutes, or until the crust is golden brown and the cheese is bubbly and slightly charred in spots.
11. Once done, remove the pizza from the oven and let it cool for a minute or two.
12. Slice the Neapolitan Pizza and serve hot.

Enjoy the authentic flavors of Neapolitan Pizza with its deliciously simple ingredients!

Four Cheese Pizza

Ingredients:

- 1 pizza dough (homemade or store-bought)
- 1/2 cup pizza sauce or marinara sauce
- 1 cup shredded mozzarella cheese
- 1/2 cup shredded fontina cheese
- 1/4 cup crumbled Gorgonzola cheese
- 1/4 cup grated Parmesan cheese
- Fresh basil leaves (optional)
- Extra-virgin olive oil
- Salt and pepper to taste
- Cornmeal or flour for dusting

Instructions:

1. Preheat your oven to the highest temperature it can go, typically around 500-550°F (260-290°C). If you have a pizza stone, place it in the oven to preheat as well.
2. Dust your work surface with cornmeal or flour to prevent sticking. Stretch or roll out the pizza dough into a circle, about 12 inches in diameter, or your desired thickness.
3. Transfer the stretched dough to a pizza peel or parchment paper dusted with cornmeal or flour.
4. Spread the pizza sauce evenly over the dough, leaving a small border around the edges.
5. Sprinkle the shredded mozzarella cheese evenly over the sauce.
6. Distribute the shredded fontina cheese over the pizza.
7. Crumble the Gorgonzola cheese and scatter it over the pizza.
8. Sprinkle the grated Parmesan cheese evenly over the pizza.
9. Season with a pinch of salt and pepper to taste.
10. Drizzle a little extra-virgin olive oil over the pizza.
11. Carefully transfer the pizza to the preheated oven, either directly onto the pizza stone or onto a baking sheet if you're using parchment paper.
12. Bake the pizza for about 10-12 minutes, or until the crust is golden brown and the cheese is bubbly and melted.
13. Once done, remove the pizza from the oven and let it cool for a minute or two.
14. Optionally, garnish with fresh basil leaves before serving.

15. Slice the Four Cheese Pizza and serve hot.

Enjoy the luxurious blend of cheeses in this decadent pizza!

Calzone

Ingredients:

For the Dough:

- 1 pound pizza dough (homemade or store-bought)
- Flour, for dusting

For the Filling:

- 1 cup ricotta cheese
- 1 cup shredded mozzarella cheese
- 1/4 cup grated Parmesan cheese
- 1/2 cup chopped cooked ham or pepperoni slices
- 1/4 cup chopped fresh basil
- 1/4 teaspoon garlic powder
- Salt and pepper, to taste

For Assembly:

- 1 egg, beaten (for egg wash)
- Marinara sauce, for serving

Instructions:

1. Preheat your oven to 450°F (230°C). If you have a pizza stone, place it in the oven to preheat as well.
2. In a mixing bowl, combine the ricotta cheese, shredded mozzarella cheese, grated Parmesan cheese, chopped ham or pepperoni, chopped fresh basil, garlic powder, salt, and pepper. Mix well to combine.
3. Divide the pizza dough into two equal portions. On a floured surface, roll out each portion of dough into a circle, about 10-12 inches in diameter.
4. Spoon the filling onto one half of each dough circle, leaving a border around the edges.
5. Fold the other half of the dough over the filling to form a half-moon shape. Press the edges together to seal, and crimp the edges with a fork.
6. Transfer the calzones to a baking sheet lined with parchment paper or a pizza peel dusted with cornmeal.
7. Brush the tops of the calzones with beaten egg to create a golden crust.

8. Using a sharp knife, make a few small slits on the top of each calzone to allow steam to escape during baking.
9. Transfer the calzones to the preheated oven and bake for 15-20 minutes, or until golden brown and crispy.
10. Remove the calzones from the oven and let them cool for a few minutes before serving.
11. Serve the calzones hot with marinara sauce for dipping.

Enjoy the deliciousness of homemade Calzone!

Prosciutto and Arugula Pizza

Ingredients:

- 1 pizza dough (homemade or store-bought)
- 1/2 cup pizza sauce or marinara sauce
- 4 oz fresh mozzarella cheese, sliced
- 2 oz thinly sliced prosciutto
- 1 cup fresh arugula
- 1 tablespoon extra-virgin olive oil
- 1/4 cup grated Parmesan cheese
- Salt and pepper to taste
- Cornmeal or flour for dusting

Instructions:

1. Preheat your oven to the highest temperature it can go, typically around 500-550°F (260-290°C). If you have a pizza stone, place it in the oven to preheat as well.
2. Dust your work surface with cornmeal or flour to prevent sticking. Stretch or roll out the pizza dough into a circle, about 12 inches in diameter, or your desired thickness.
3. Transfer the stretched dough to a pizza peel or parchment paper dusted with cornmeal or flour.
4. Spread the pizza sauce evenly over the dough, leaving a small border around the edges.
5. Arrange the sliced fresh mozzarella cheese evenly over the sauce.
6. Tear the prosciutto into smaller pieces and scatter them over the cheese.
7. Drizzle a little extra-virgin olive oil over the pizza.
8. Sprinkle grated Parmesan cheese over the pizza.
9. Season with salt and pepper to taste.
10. Carefully transfer the pizza to the preheated oven, either directly onto the pizza stone or onto a baking sheet if you're using parchment paper.
11. Bake the pizza for about 10-12 minutes, or until the crust is golden brown and the cheese is bubbly and slightly browned.
12. Once done, remove the pizza from the oven and let it cool for a minute or two.
13. Scatter fresh arugula over the pizza.
14. Slice the Prosciutto and Arugula Pizza and serve hot.

Enjoy the wonderful flavors of this gourmet pizza!

Capricciosa Pizza

Ingredients:

- 1 pizza dough (homemade or store-bought)
- 1/2 cup pizza sauce or marinara sauce
- 1 cup shredded mozzarella cheese
- 2 oz cooked ham, sliced or diced
- 1/2 cup canned artichoke hearts, drained and quartered
- 1/2 cup sliced mushrooms
- 1/4 cup sliced black olives
- Fresh basil leaves (optional)
- Extra-virgin olive oil
- Salt and pepper to taste
- Cornmeal or flour for dusting

Instructions:

1. Preheat your oven to the highest temperature it can go, typically around 500-550°F (260-290°C). If you have a pizza stone, place it in the oven to preheat as well.
2. Dust your work surface with cornmeal or flour to prevent sticking. Stretch or roll out the pizza dough into a circle, about 12 inches in diameter, or your desired thickness.
3. Transfer the stretched dough to a pizza peel or parchment paper dusted with cornmeal or flour.
4. Spread the pizza sauce evenly over the dough, leaving a small border around the edges.
5. Sprinkle the shredded mozzarella cheese evenly over the sauce.
6. Arrange the sliced or diced cooked ham over the cheese.
7. Distribute the quartered artichoke hearts, sliced mushrooms, and sliced black olives over the pizza.
8. Drizzle a little extra-virgin olive oil over the pizza.
9. Season with salt and pepper to taste.
10. Carefully transfer the pizza to the preheated oven, either directly onto the pizza stone or onto a baking sheet if you're using parchment paper.
11. Bake the pizza for about 10-12 minutes, or until the crust is golden brown and the cheese is bubbly and melted.
12. Once done, remove the pizza from the oven and let it cool for a minute or two.

13. Optionally, garnish with fresh basil leaves before serving.
14. Slice the Capricciosa Pizza and serve hot.

Enjoy the delicious blend of flavors in this classic Italian pizza!

Quattro Stagioni Pizza

Ingredients:

- 1 pizza dough (homemade or store-bought)
- 1/2 cup pizza sauce or marinara sauce
- 1 cup shredded mozzarella cheese
- 2 oz cooked ham, diced
- 4-6 canned artichoke hearts, drained and quartered
- 1/2 cup sliced mushrooms
- 1/4 cup sliced black olives
- 1/4 cup diced bell peppers (red, green, or yellow)
- 4 cherry tomatoes, halved
- Fresh basil leaves (optional)
- Extra-virgin olive oil
- Salt and pepper to taste
- Cornmeal or flour for dusting

Instructions:

1. Preheat your oven to the highest temperature it can go, typically around 500-550°F (260-290°C). If you have a pizza stone, place it in the oven to preheat as well.
2. Dust your work surface with cornmeal or flour to prevent sticking. Stretch or roll out the pizza dough into a circle, about 12 inches in diameter, or your desired thickness.
3. Transfer the stretched dough to a pizza peel or parchment paper dusted with cornmeal or flour.
4. Divide the pizza dough into four equal sections.
5. Spread the pizza sauce evenly over each quadrant of the dough, leaving a small border around the edges.
6. Sprinkle the shredded mozzarella cheese evenly over each section of sauce.
7. In the first quadrant, arrange the diced ham.
8. In the second quadrant, distribute the quartered artichoke hearts.
9. In the third quadrant, spread the sliced mushrooms.
10. In the fourth quadrant, scatter the sliced black olives and diced bell peppers.
11. Place two cherry tomato halves in each quadrant.
12. Drizzle a little extra-virgin olive oil over the entire pizza.
13. Season each quadrant with salt and pepper to taste.

14. Carefully transfer the pizza to the preheated oven, either directly onto the pizza stone or onto a baking sheet if you're using parchment paper.
15. Bake the pizza for about 10-12 minutes, or until the crust is golden brown and the cheese is bubbly and melted.
16. Once done, remove the pizza from the oven and let it cool for a minute or two.
17. Optionally, garnish with fresh basil leaves before serving.
18. Slice the Quattro Stagioni Pizza and serve hot.

Enjoy the delicious flavors of each season in this unique pizza!

Sicilian Pizza

Ingredients:

For the Dough:

- 4 cups all-purpose flour
- 1 1/4 cups warm water
- 2 teaspoons active dry yeast
- 2 tablespoons olive oil
- 1 teaspoon sugar
- 1 teaspoon salt

For the Toppings:

- 1 1/2 cups pizza sauce or marinara sauce
- 2 cups shredded mozzarella cheese
- 1/2 cup grated Parmesan cheese
- 1/4 cup sliced pepperoni or cooked Italian sausage (optional)
- 1/4 cup sliced black olives (optional)
- 1/4 cup sliced mushrooms (optional)
- Fresh basil leaves (optional)
- Extra-virgin olive oil
- Salt and pepper to taste
- Cornmeal or flour for dusting

Instructions:

1. In a small bowl, dissolve the sugar in warm water. Sprinkle the yeast over the water and let it sit for about 5-10 minutes, until frothy.
2. In a large mixing bowl, combine the flour and salt. Make a well in the center and pour in the yeast mixture and olive oil. Stir until a dough forms.
3. Turn the dough out onto a floured surface and knead for about 5-7 minutes, until smooth and elastic. Shape the dough into a ball.
4. Place the dough in a lightly oiled bowl, cover with a clean kitchen towel or plastic wrap, and let it rise in a warm place for about 1-2 hours, until doubled in size.
5. Preheat your oven to 425°F (220°C). Grease a 9x13-inch baking pan with olive oil and sprinkle with cornmeal or flour.
6. Punch down the risen dough and transfer it to the prepared baking pan. Press the dough evenly into the pan, spreading it to the edges.

7. Cover the dough with a clean kitchen towel and let it rest for another 15-20 minutes.
8. Once rested, spread the pizza sauce evenly over the dough, leaving a small border around the edges.
9. Sprinkle the shredded mozzarella cheese evenly over the sauce.
10. If using, distribute the sliced pepperoni or cooked Italian sausage, sliced black olives, and sliced mushrooms over the cheese.
11. Drizzle a little extra-virgin olive oil over the pizza.
12. Season with salt and pepper to taste.
13. Bake the pizza in the preheated oven for 20-25 minutes, or until the crust is golden brown and the cheese is bubbly and melted.
14. Once done, remove the pizza from the oven and let it cool for a few minutes.
15. Optionally, garnish with fresh basil leaves before serving.
16. Slice the Sicilian Pizza into squares and serve hot.

Enjoy the thick and fluffy goodness of Sicilian Pizza!

White Pizza with Garlic and Mushrooms

Ingredients:

For the Pizza Dough:

- 1 pound pizza dough (homemade or store-bought)
- Flour, for dusting

For the White Sauce:

- 2 tablespoons unsalted butter
- 2 tablespoons all-purpose flour
- 1 cup whole milk
- 1/2 cup grated Parmesan cheese
- 2 cloves garlic, minced
- Salt and pepper to taste

For the Toppings:

- 1 cup shredded mozzarella cheese
- 1 cup sliced mushrooms (such as cremini or button mushrooms)
- 2 cloves garlic, thinly sliced
- 2 tablespoons extra-virgin olive oil
- Fresh parsley, chopped (for garnish)
- Red pepper flakes (optional)

Instructions:

1. Preheat your oven to 475°F (245°C). If you have a pizza stone, place it in the oven to preheat as well.
2. In a small saucepan, melt the butter over medium heat. Add the minced garlic and cook for 1-2 minutes until fragrant.
3. Stir in the flour and cook for another 1-2 minutes to make a roux.
4. Gradually whisk in the milk, stirring constantly to prevent lumps from forming. Cook the sauce until it thickens, about 2-3 minutes.
5. Remove the saucepan from the heat and stir in the grated Parmesan cheese until melted and smooth. Season with salt and pepper to taste. Set aside.
6. In a skillet, heat the olive oil over medium heat. Add the sliced mushrooms and garlic, and sauté until the mushrooms are tender and golden brown, about 5-7 minutes. Season with salt and pepper to taste. Remove from heat and set aside.

7. On a lightly floured surface, roll out the pizza dough into a circle or rectangle, about 1/4 inch thick.
8. Transfer the rolled-out dough to a baking sheet or pizza peel dusted with cornmeal or flour.
9. Spread the white sauce evenly over the dough, leaving a small border around the edges.
10. Sprinkle the shredded mozzarella cheese over the sauce.
11. Distribute the sautéed mushrooms and garlic evenly over the cheese.
12. Drizzle a little extra-virgin olive oil over the pizza.
13. Transfer the pizza to the preheated oven and bake for 12-15 minutes, or until the crust is golden brown and the cheese is bubbly and melted.
14. Once done, remove the pizza from the oven and let it cool for a minute or two.
15. Garnish with chopped fresh parsley and red pepper flakes (if using) before serving.
16. Slice the White Pizza with Garlic and Mushrooms and serve hot.

Enjoy the delicious combination of flavors in this white pizza!

Focaccia Pizza

Ingredients:

For the Focaccia Dough:

- 3 cups all-purpose flour
- 1 1/4 cups warm water
- 2 teaspoons active dry yeast
- 2 tablespoons olive oil
- 1 teaspoon salt
- 1 teaspoon sugar

For the Toppings:

- 1/2 cup pizza sauce or marinara sauce
- 2 cups shredded mozzarella cheese
- 1/4 cup sliced pepperoni or cooked Italian sausage (optional)
- 1/4 cup sliced black olives
- 1/4 cup sliced red onion
- 1/4 cup sliced bell peppers (red, green, or yellow)
- Fresh basil leaves (optional)
- Extra-virgin olive oil
- Salt and pepper to taste
- Cornmeal or flour for dusting

Instructions:

1. In a small bowl, dissolve the sugar in warm water. Sprinkle the yeast over the water and let it sit for about 5-10 minutes, until frothy.
2. In a large mixing bowl, combine the flour and salt. Make a well in the center and pour in the yeast mixture and olive oil. Stir until a dough forms.
3. Turn the dough out onto a floured surface and knead for about 5-7 minutes, until smooth and elastic. Shape the dough into a ball.
4. Place the dough in a lightly oiled bowl, cover with a clean kitchen towel or plastic wrap, and let it rise in a warm place for about 1-2 hours, until doubled in size.
5. Preheat your oven to 425°F (220°C). Grease a 9x13-inch baking pan with olive oil and sprinkle with cornmeal or flour.
6. Punch down the risen dough and transfer it to the prepared baking pan. Press the dough evenly into the pan, spreading it to the edges.

7. Cover the dough with a clean kitchen towel and let it rest for another 15-20 minutes.
8. Once rested, spread the pizza sauce evenly over the dough, leaving a small border around the edges.
9. Sprinkle the shredded mozzarella cheese evenly over the sauce.
10. If using, distribute the sliced pepperoni or cooked Italian sausage, sliced black olives, sliced red onion, and sliced bell peppers over the cheese.
11. Drizzle a little extra-virgin olive oil over the pizza.
12. Season with salt and pepper to taste.
13. Bake the pizza in the preheated oven for 20-25 minutes, or until the crust is golden brown and the cheese is bubbly and melted.
14. Once done, remove the pizza from the oven and let it cool for a few minutes.
15. Optionally, garnish with fresh basil leaves before serving.
16. Slice the Focaccia Pizza into squares and serve hot.

Enjoy the deliciousness of Focaccia Pizza with its fluffy crust and flavorful toppings!

Fig and Goat Cheese Pizza

Ingredients:

- 1 pizza dough (homemade or store-bought)
- 6-8 fresh figs, sliced
- 4 oz goat cheese, crumbled
- 2 tablespoons honey
- 1/4 cup chopped walnuts or pecans
- Fresh arugula (optional, for garnish)
- Extra-virgin olive oil
- Salt and pepper to taste

Instructions:

1. Preheat your oven to the highest temperature it can go, typically around 500-550°F (260-290°C). If you have a pizza stone, place it in the oven to preheat as well.
2. Dust your work surface with cornmeal or flour to prevent sticking. Stretch or roll out the pizza dough into a circle, about 12 inches in diameter, or your desired thickness.
3. Transfer the stretched dough to a pizza peel or parchment paper dusted with cornmeal or flour.
4. Drizzle a little extra-virgin olive oil over the dough and spread it evenly with your hands.
5. Arrange the sliced figs evenly over the dough.
6. Crumble the goat cheese over the figs.
7. Drizzle the honey over the pizza.
8. Sprinkle the chopped walnuts or pecans over the pizza.
9. Season with a pinch of salt and pepper to taste.
10. Carefully transfer the pizza to the preheated oven, either directly onto the pizza stone or onto a baking sheet if you're using parchment paper.
11. Bake the pizza for about 10-12 minutes, or until the crust is golden brown and the cheese is melted and bubbly.
12. Once done, remove the pizza from the oven and let it cool for a minute or two.
13. Optionally, garnish with fresh arugula before serving.
14. Slice the Fig and Goat Cheese Pizza and serve hot.

Enjoy the delicious combination of flavors in this unique pizza!

Pesto Pizza

Ingredients:

- 1 pizza dough (homemade or store-bought)
- 1/2 cup basil pesto sauce (homemade or store-bought)
- 1 cup shredded mozzarella cheese
- 1/4 cup grated Parmesan cheese
- 1/4 cup sun-dried tomatoes, thinly sliced
- 1/4 cup sliced black olives
- Fresh basil leaves, thinly sliced (for garnish)
- Extra-virgin olive oil
- Salt and pepper to taste
- Cornmeal or flour for dusting

Instructions:

1. Preheat your oven to the highest temperature it can go, typically around 500-550°F (260-290°C). If you have a pizza stone, place it in the oven to preheat as well.
2. Dust your work surface with cornmeal or flour to prevent sticking. Stretch or roll out the pizza dough into a circle, about 12 inches in diameter, or your desired thickness.
3. Transfer the stretched dough to a pizza peel or parchment paper dusted with cornmeal or flour.
4. Spread the basil pesto sauce evenly over the dough, leaving a small border around the edges.
5. Sprinkle the shredded mozzarella cheese evenly over the pesto sauce.
6. Scatter the sliced sun-dried tomatoes and sliced black olives over the cheese.
7. Sprinkle the grated Parmesan cheese evenly over the pizza.
8. Drizzle a little extra-virgin olive oil over the pizza.
9. Season with salt and pepper to taste.
10. Carefully transfer the pizza to the preheated oven, either directly onto the pizza stone or onto a baking sheet if you're using parchment paper.
11. Bake the pizza for about 10-12 minutes, or until the crust is golden brown and the cheese is bubbly and melted.
12. Once done, remove the pizza from the oven and let it cool for a minute or two.
13. Garnish with thinly sliced fresh basil leaves before serving.
14. Slice the Pesto Pizza and serve hot.

Enjoy the delicious and aromatic flavors of this Pesto Pizza!

Sausage and Peppers Pizza

Ingredients:

- 1 pizza dough (homemade or store-bought)
- 1/2 cup pizza sauce or marinara sauce
- 1 1/2 cups shredded mozzarella cheese
- 1/2 pound Italian sausage, casings removed and crumbled
- 1 bell pepper, thinly sliced (any color you prefer)
- 1/2 onion, thinly sliced
- 2 cloves garlic, minced
- 1 tablespoon olive oil
- Salt and pepper to taste
- Red pepper flakes (optional)
- Fresh basil leaves (optional)
- Cornmeal or flour for dusting

Instructions:

1. Preheat your oven to the highest temperature it can go, typically around 500-550°F (260-290°C). If you have a pizza stone, place it in the oven to preheat as well.
2. In a skillet, heat the olive oil over medium heat. Add the crumbled Italian sausage and cook until browned and cooked through, breaking it up with a spoon as it cooks. Remove the cooked sausage from the skillet and set it aside.
3. In the same skillet, add the sliced bell pepper and onion. Cook until the vegetables are softened and slightly caramelized, about 5-7 minutes. Add the minced garlic and cook for an additional 1-2 minutes. Season with salt and pepper to taste. Remove the skillet from heat and set aside.
4. Dust your work surface with cornmeal or flour to prevent sticking. Stretch or roll out the pizza dough into a circle, about 12 inches in diameter, or your desired thickness.
5. Transfer the stretched dough to a pizza peel or parchment paper dusted with cornmeal or flour.
6. Spread the pizza sauce evenly over the dough, leaving a small border around the edges.
7. Sprinkle the shredded mozzarella cheese evenly over the sauce.
8. Distribute the cooked Italian sausage, sautéed bell pepper, and onion mixture evenly over the cheese.

9. Optionally, sprinkle red pepper flakes over the pizza for extra heat.
10. Carefully transfer the pizza to the preheated oven, either directly onto the pizza stone or onto a baking sheet if you're using parchment paper.
11. Bake the pizza for about 10-12 minutes, or until the crust is golden brown and the cheese is bubbly and melted.
12. Once done, remove the pizza from the oven and let it cool for a minute or two.
13. Optionally, garnish with fresh basil leaves before serving.
14. Slice the Sausage and Peppers Pizza and serve hot.

Enjoy the delicious combination of flavors in this classic pizza!

Spinach and Ricotta Pizza

Ingredients:

- 1 pizza dough (homemade or store-bought)
- 1/2 cup pizza sauce or marinara sauce
- 1 cup shredded mozzarella cheese
- 1 cup fresh spinach leaves, roughly chopped
- 1/2 cup ricotta cheese
- 2 cloves garlic, minced
- 2 tablespoons olive oil
- Salt and pepper to taste
- Red pepper flakes (optional)
- Cornmeal or flour for dusting

Instructions:

1. Preheat your oven to the highest temperature it can go, typically around 500-550°F (260-290°C). If you have a pizza stone, place it in the oven to preheat as well.
2. In a skillet, heat the olive oil over medium heat. Add the minced garlic and cook for 1-2 minutes until fragrant. Add the chopped spinach leaves and cook until wilted, about 2-3 minutes. Season with salt and pepper to taste. Remove from heat and set aside.
3. Dust your work surface with cornmeal or flour to prevent sticking. Stretch or roll out the pizza dough into a circle, about 12 inches in diameter, or your desired thickness.
4. Transfer the stretched dough to a pizza peel or parchment paper dusted with cornmeal or flour.
5. Spread the pizza sauce evenly over the dough, leaving a small border around the edges.
6. Sprinkle the shredded mozzarella cheese evenly over the sauce.
7. Dollop spoonfuls of ricotta cheese over the pizza.
8. Distribute the cooked spinach and garlic mixture evenly over the cheese.
9. Optionally, sprinkle red pepper flakes over the pizza for extra heat.
10. Carefully transfer the pizza to the preheated oven, either directly onto the pizza stone or onto a baking sheet if you're using parchment paper.
11. Bake the pizza for about 10-12 minutes, or until the crust is golden brown and the cheese is bubbly and melted.

12. Once done, remove the pizza from the oven and let it cool for a minute or two.
13. Slice the Spinach and Ricotta Pizza and serve hot.

Enjoy the deliciousness of this vegetarian pizza!

Eggplant Parmesan Pizza

Ingredients:

For the Eggplant:

- 1 medium eggplant, thinly sliced
- 1 cup breadcrumbs
- 1/2 cup grated Parmesan cheese
- 2 eggs, beaten
- Salt and pepper to taste
- Olive oil for frying

For the Pizza:

- 1 pizza dough (homemade or store-bought)
- 1/2 cup pizza sauce or marinara sauce
- 1 1/2 cups shredded mozzarella cheese
- 1/4 cup grated Parmesan cheese
- Fresh basil leaves, torn (for garnish)
- Crushed red pepper flakes (optional)

Instructions:

1. Preheat your oven to the highest temperature it can go, typically around 500-550°F (260-290°C). If you have a pizza stone, place it in the oven to preheat as well.
2. Prepare the eggplant: Season the eggplant slices with salt and pepper. In a shallow dish, combine the breadcrumbs and grated Parmesan cheese. Dip each eggplant slice in the beaten eggs, then coat with the breadcrumb mixture.
3. In a skillet, heat olive oil over medium-high heat. Fry the breaded eggplant slices until golden brown and crispy, about 2-3 minutes per side. Transfer the fried eggplant slices to a paper towel-lined plate to drain any excess oil.
4. Dust your work surface with cornmeal or flour to prevent sticking. Stretch or roll out the pizza dough into a circle, about 12 inches in diameter, or your desired thickness.
5. Transfer the stretched dough to a pizza peel or parchment paper dusted with cornmeal or flour.
6. Spread the pizza sauce evenly over the dough, leaving a small border around the edges.

7. Sprinkle the shredded mozzarella cheese evenly over the sauce.
8. Arrange the fried eggplant slices evenly over the cheese.
9. Sprinkle the grated Parmesan cheese over the pizza.
10. Carefully transfer the pizza to the preheated oven, either directly onto the pizza stone or onto a baking sheet if you're using parchment paper.
11. Bake the pizza for about 10-12 minutes, or until the crust is golden brown and the cheese is bubbly and melted.
12. Once done, remove the pizza from the oven and let it cool for a minute or two.
13. Garnish with torn fresh basil leaves and crushed red pepper flakes (if using) before serving.
14. Slice the Eggplant Parmesan Pizza and serve hot.

Enjoy the delicious fusion of flavors in this unique pizza!

Gorgonzola and Pear Pizza

Ingredients:

- 1 pizza dough (homemade or store-bought)
- 1/2 cup crumbled Gorgonzola cheese
- 1 ripe pear, thinly sliced
- 1/4 cup chopped walnuts
- 1 tablespoon honey
- 2 tablespoons balsamic glaze (optional)
- Fresh thyme leaves (optional, for garnish)
- Olive oil for drizzling
- Salt and pepper to taste
- Cornmeal or flour for dusting

Instructions:

1. Preheat your oven to the highest temperature it can go, typically around 500-550°F (260-290°C). If you have a pizza stone, place it in the oven to preheat as well.
2. Dust your work surface with cornmeal or flour to prevent sticking. Stretch or roll out the pizza dough into a circle, about 12 inches in diameter, or your desired thickness.
3. Transfer the stretched dough to a pizza peel or parchment paper dusted with cornmeal or flour.
4. Drizzle a little olive oil over the dough and spread it evenly with your hands.
5. Sprinkle the crumbled Gorgonzola cheese evenly over the dough.
6. Arrange the thinly sliced pear over the cheese.
7. Sprinkle the chopped walnuts over the pizza.
8. Drizzle the honey over the pizza.
9. Season with a pinch of salt and pepper to taste.
10. Carefully transfer the pizza to the preheated oven, either directly onto the pizza stone or onto a baking sheet if you're using parchment paper.
11. Bake the pizza for about 10-12 minutes, or until the crust is golden brown and the cheese is bubbly and melted.
12. Once done, remove the pizza from the oven and let it cool for a minute or two.
13. Drizzle the balsamic glaze (if using) over the pizza.
14. Optionally, garnish with fresh thyme leaves before serving.
15. Slice the Gorgonzola and Pear Pizza and serve hot.

Enjoy the delicious combination of flavors in this unique pizza!

Zucchini and Feta Pizza

Ingredients:

- 1 pizza dough (homemade or store-bought)
- 1 medium zucchini, thinly sliced
- 1/2 cup crumbled feta cheese
- 1/4 cup sliced black olives
- 2 tablespoons chopped fresh basil
- 2 cloves garlic, minced
- 2 tablespoons extra-virgin olive oil
- Salt and pepper to taste
- Cornmeal or flour for dusting

Instructions:

1. Preheat your oven to the highest temperature it can go, typically around 500-550°F (260-290°C). If you have a pizza stone, place it in the oven to preheat as well.
2. In a skillet, heat 1 tablespoon of olive oil over medium heat. Add the minced garlic and cook for 1-2 minutes until fragrant. Add the thinly sliced zucchini to the skillet and sauté until tender, about 5-7 minutes. Season with salt and pepper to taste. Remove from heat and set aside.
3. Dust your work surface with cornmeal or flour to prevent sticking. Stretch or roll out the pizza dough into a circle, about 12 inches in diameter, or your desired thickness.
4. Transfer the stretched dough to a pizza peel or parchment paper dusted with cornmeal or flour.
5. Drizzle the remaining tablespoon of olive oil over the dough and spread it evenly with your hands.
6. Sprinkle the crumbled feta cheese evenly over the dough.
7. Arrange the sautéed zucchini slices over the cheese.
8. Scatter the sliced black olives over the pizza.
9. Sprinkle the chopped fresh basil over the pizza.
10. Season with a pinch of salt and pepper to taste.
11. Carefully transfer the pizza to the preheated oven, either directly onto the pizza stone or onto a baking sheet if you're using parchment paper.
12. Bake the pizza for about 10-12 minutes, or until the crust is golden brown and the cheese is bubbly and melted.

13. Once done, remove the pizza from the oven and let it cool for a minute or two.
14. Slice the Zucchini and Feta Pizza and serve hot.

Enjoy the fresh and savory flavors of this delicious pizza!

Caramelized Onion and Brie Pizza

Ingredients:

- 1 pizza dough (homemade or store-bought)
- 2 large onions, thinly sliced
- 2 tablespoons butter
- 1 tablespoon olive oil
- 1 tablespoon balsamic vinegar
- Salt and pepper to taste
- 8 oz Brie cheese, thinly sliced
- Fresh thyme leaves (optional, for garnish)
- Cornmeal or flour for dusting

Instructions:

1. Preheat your oven to the highest temperature it can go, typically around 500-550°F (260-290°C). If you have a pizza stone, place it in the oven to preheat as well.
2. In a large skillet, heat the butter and olive oil over medium heat. Add the thinly sliced onions and cook, stirring occasionally, until they are soft and caramelized, about 20-25 minutes.
3. Stir in the balsamic vinegar and continue cooking for another 5 minutes until the onions are deeply caramelized. Season with salt and pepper to taste. Remove from heat and set aside.
4. Dust your work surface with cornmeal or flour to prevent sticking. Stretch or roll out the pizza dough into a circle, about 12 inches in diameter, or your desired thickness.
5. Transfer the stretched dough to a pizza peel or parchment paper dusted with cornmeal or flour.
6. Spread the caramelized onions evenly over the dough, leaving a small border around the edges.
7. Arrange the thinly sliced Brie cheese over the onions.
8. Carefully transfer the pizza to the preheated oven, either directly onto the pizza stone or onto a baking sheet if you're using parchment paper.
9. Bake the pizza for about 10-12 minutes, or until the crust is golden brown and the cheese is melted and bubbly.
10. Once done, remove the pizza from the oven and let it cool for a minute or two.
11. Optionally, garnish with fresh thyme leaves before serving.

12. Slice the Caramelized Onion and Brie Pizza and serve hot.

Enjoy the rich and flavorful taste of this unique pizza!

Roasted Red Pepper and Goat Cheese Pizza

Ingredients:

- 1 pizza dough (homemade or store-bought)
- 1 cup roasted red peppers, sliced
- 4 oz goat cheese, crumbled
- 1/4 cup sliced black olives
- 2 cloves garlic, minced
- 2 tablespoons extra-virgin olive oil
- Salt and pepper to taste
- Fresh basil leaves, torn (for garnish)
- Crushed red pepper flakes (optional)
- Cornmeal or flour for dusting

Instructions:

1. Preheat your oven to the highest temperature it can go, typically around 500-550°F (260-290°C). If you have a pizza stone, place it in the oven to preheat as well.
2. Dust your work surface with cornmeal or flour to prevent sticking. Stretch or roll out the pizza dough into a circle, about 12 inches in diameter, or your desired thickness.
3. Transfer the stretched dough to a pizza peel or parchment paper dusted with cornmeal or flour.
4. In a small bowl, mix the minced garlic with the extra-virgin olive oil.
5. Brush the garlic-infused olive oil evenly over the surface of the pizza dough.
6. Spread the sliced roasted red peppers evenly over the dough.
7. Scatter the crumbled goat cheese and sliced black olives over the peppers.
8. Season the pizza with salt and pepper to taste.
9. Optionally, sprinkle crushed red pepper flakes over the pizza for some heat.
10. Carefully transfer the pizza to the preheated oven, either directly onto the pizza stone or onto a baking sheet if you're using parchment paper.
11. Bake the pizza for about 10-12 minutes, or until the crust is golden brown and the cheese is bubbly and melted.
12. Once done, remove the pizza from the oven and let it cool for a minute or two.
13. Garnish with torn fresh basil leaves before serving.
14. Slice the Roasted Red Pepper and Goat Cheese Pizza and serve hot.

Enjoy the delicious combination of flavors in this unique pizza!

Margherita with Balsamic Glaze Drizzle

Ingredients:

- 1 pizza dough (homemade or store-bought)
- 1/2 cup pizza sauce or marinara sauce
- 1 1/2 cups shredded mozzarella cheese
- 2-3 ripe tomatoes, thinly sliced
- Fresh basil leaves
- Balsamic glaze
- Salt and pepper to taste
- Extra-virgin olive oil
- Cornmeal or flour for dusting

Instructions:

1. Preheat your oven to the highest temperature it can go, typically around 500-550°F (260-290°C). If you have a pizza stone, place it in the oven to preheat as well.
2. Dust your work surface with cornmeal or flour to prevent sticking. Stretch or roll out the pizza dough into a circle, about 12 inches in diameter, or your desired thickness.
3. Transfer the stretched dough to a pizza peel or parchment paper dusted with cornmeal or flour.
4. Spread the pizza sauce evenly over the dough, leaving a small border around the edges.
5. Sprinkle the shredded mozzarella cheese evenly over the sauce.
6. Arrange the thinly sliced tomatoes over the cheese.
7. Tear fresh basil leaves and scatter them over the pizza.
8. Drizzle a little extra-virgin olive oil over the pizza.
9. Season with salt and pepper to taste.
10. Carefully transfer the pizza to the preheated oven, either directly onto the pizza stone or onto a baking sheet if you're using parchment paper.
11. Bake the pizza for about 10-12 minutes, or until the crust is golden brown and the cheese is bubbly and melted.
12. Once done, remove the pizza from the oven and let it cool for a minute or two.
13. Drizzle balsamic glaze over the pizza in a zigzag pattern.
14. Slice the Margherita Pizza with Balsamic Glaze Drizzle and serve hot.

Enjoy the sweet and tangy flavor addition to this classic pizza!

Rustic Chicken Alfredo Pizza

Ingredients:

- 1 pizza dough (homemade or store-bought)
- 1 cup cooked chicken breast, diced or shredded
- 1 cup Alfredo sauce (homemade or store-bought)
- 1 1/2 cups shredded mozzarella cheese
- 1/4 cup grated Parmesan cheese
- 2 cloves garlic, minced
- 2 tablespoons butter
- Salt and pepper to taste
- Fresh parsley, chopped (for garnish)
- Olive oil for drizzling
- Cornmeal or flour for dusting

Instructions:

1. Preheat your oven to the highest temperature it can go, typically around 500-550°F (260-290°C). If you have a pizza stone, place it in the oven to preheat as well.
2. In a small skillet, melt the butter over medium heat. Add the minced garlic and cook for 1-2 minutes until fragrant. Add the cooked chicken breast to the skillet and toss until heated through. Season with salt and pepper to taste. Remove from heat and set aside.
3. Dust your work surface with cornmeal or flour to prevent sticking. Stretch or roll out the pizza dough into a circle, about 12 inches in diameter, or your desired thickness.
4. Transfer the stretched dough to a pizza peel or parchment paper dusted with cornmeal or flour.
5. Spread the Alfredo sauce evenly over the dough, leaving a small border around the edges.
6. Sprinkle the shredded mozzarella cheese evenly over the sauce.
7. Arrange the cooked chicken breast over the cheese.
8. Sprinkle the grated Parmesan cheese over the pizza.
9. Drizzle a little olive oil over the pizza.
10. Carefully transfer the pizza to the preheated oven, either directly onto the pizza stone or onto a baking sheet if you're using parchment paper.

11. Bake the pizza for about 10-12 minutes, or until the crust is golden brown and the cheese is bubbly and melted.
12. Once done, remove the pizza from the oven and let it cool for a minute or two.
13. Garnish with chopped fresh parsley before serving.
14. Slice the Rustic Chicken Alfredo Pizza and serve hot.

Enjoy the creamy and savory flavors of this delicious pizza!

Margherita with Fresh Basil and Cherry Tomatoes

Ingredients:

- 1 pizza dough (homemade or store-bought)
- 1/2 cup pizza sauce or marinara sauce
- 1 1/2 cups shredded mozzarella cheese
- 1 cup cherry tomatoes, halved
- Fresh basil leaves
- Extra-virgin olive oil
- Salt and pepper to taste
- Cornmeal or flour for dusting

Instructions:

1. Preheat your oven to the highest temperature it can go, typically around 500-550°F (260-290°C). If you have a pizza stone, place it in the oven to preheat as well.
2. Dust your work surface with cornmeal or flour to prevent sticking. Stretch or roll out the pizza dough into a circle, about 12 inches in diameter, or your desired thickness.
3. Transfer the stretched dough to a pizza peel or parchment paper dusted with cornmeal or flour.
4. Spread the pizza sauce evenly over the dough, leaving a small border around the edges.
5. Sprinkle the shredded mozzarella cheese evenly over the sauce.
6. Arrange the halved cherry tomatoes over the cheese.
7. Tear fresh basil leaves and scatter them over the pizza.
8. Drizzle a little extra-virgin olive oil over the pizza.
9. Season with salt and pepper to taste.
10. Carefully transfer the pizza to the preheated oven, either directly onto the pizza stone or onto a baking sheet if you're using parchment paper.
11. Bake the pizza for about 10-12 minutes, or until the crust is golden brown and the cheese is bubbly and melted.
12. Once done, remove the pizza from the oven and let it cool for a minute or two.
13. Slice the Margherita Pizza with Fresh Basil and Cherry Tomatoes and serve hot.

Enjoy the fresh and vibrant flavors of this delicious pizza!

Italian Sausage and Kale Pizza

Ingredients:

- 1 pizza dough (homemade or store-bought)
- 1/2 cup pizza sauce or marinara sauce
- 1 1/2 cups shredded mozzarella cheese
- 1/2 pound Italian sausage, casings removed
- 2 cups kale, chopped
- 2 cloves garlic, minced
- 1 tablespoon olive oil
- Salt and pepper to taste
- Red pepper flakes (optional)
- Grated Parmesan cheese (optional)
- Cornmeal or flour for dusting

Instructions:

1. Preheat your oven to the highest temperature it can go, typically around 500-550°F (260-290°C). If you have a pizza stone, place it in the oven to preheat as well.
2. In a skillet, heat olive oil over medium heat. Add the minced garlic and cook for 1-2 minutes until fragrant. Add the Italian sausage to the skillet and cook until browned and cooked through, breaking it up with a spoon as it cooks. Remove the sausage from the skillet and set it aside.
3. In the same skillet, add the chopped kale and cook until wilted, about 3-4 minutes. Season with salt and pepper to taste. Remove from heat and set aside.
4. Dust your work surface with cornmeal or flour to prevent sticking. Stretch or roll out the pizza dough into a circle, about 12 inches in diameter, or your desired thickness.
5. Transfer the stretched dough to a pizza peel or parchment paper dusted with cornmeal or flour.
6. Spread the pizza sauce evenly over the dough, leaving a small border around the edges.
7. Sprinkle the shredded mozzarella cheese evenly over the sauce.
8. Distribute the cooked Italian sausage and wilted kale evenly over the cheese.
9. Optionally, sprinkle red pepper flakes over the pizza for some heat.
10. Carefully transfer the pizza to the preheated oven, either directly onto the pizza stone or onto a baking sheet if you're using parchment paper.

11. Bake the pizza for about 10-12 minutes, or until the crust is golden brown and the cheese is bubbly and melted.
12. Once done, remove the pizza from the oven and let it cool for a minute or two.
13. Optionally, sprinkle grated Parmesan cheese over the pizza before serving.
14. Slice the Italian Sausage and Kale Pizza and serve hot.

Enjoy the delicious and hearty flavors of this pizza!

Mediterranean Veggie Pizza

Ingredients:

- 1 pizza dough (homemade or store-bought)
- 1/2 cup pizza sauce or marinara sauce
- 1 1/2 cups shredded mozzarella cheese
- 1/2 cup cherry tomatoes, halved
- 1/2 cup sliced black olives
- 1/4 cup sliced red onion
- 1/4 cup chopped roasted red peppers
- 1/4 cup crumbled feta cheese
- 2 tablespoons chopped fresh basil
- 2 tablespoons extra-virgin olive oil
- 2 cloves garlic, minced
- Salt and pepper to taste
- Cornmeal or flour for dusting

Instructions:

1. Preheat your oven to the highest temperature it can go, typically around 500-550°F (260-290°C). If you have a pizza stone, place it in the oven to preheat as well.
2. In a small skillet, heat the extra-virgin olive oil over medium heat. Add the minced garlic and cook for 1-2 minutes until fragrant. Remove from heat and set aside.
3. Dust your work surface with cornmeal or flour to prevent sticking. Stretch or roll out the pizza dough into a circle, about 12 inches in diameter, or your desired thickness.
4. Transfer the stretched dough to a pizza peel or parchment paper dusted with cornmeal or flour.
5. Brush the garlic-infused olive oil evenly over the surface of the pizza dough.
6. Spread the pizza sauce evenly over the dough, leaving a small border around the edges.
7. Sprinkle the shredded mozzarella cheese evenly over the sauce.
8. Arrange the halved cherry tomatoes, sliced black olives, sliced red onion, and chopped roasted red peppers over the cheese.
9. Sprinkle the crumbled feta cheese over the pizza.
10. Season with salt and pepper to taste.

11. Carefully transfer the pizza to the preheated oven, either directly onto the pizza stone or onto a baking sheet if you're using parchment paper.
12. Bake the pizza for about 10-12 minutes, or until the crust is golden brown and the cheese is bubbly and melted.
13. Once done, remove the pizza from the oven and let it cool for a minute or two.
14. Sprinkle the chopped fresh basil over the pizza before serving.
15. Slice the Mediterranean Veggie Pizza and serve hot.

Enjoy the vibrant and delicious flavors of this Mediterranean-inspired pizza!

Artichoke and Sun-Dried Tomato Pizza

Ingredients:

- 1 pizza dough (homemade or store-bought)
- 1/2 cup pizza sauce or marinara sauce
- 1 1/2 cups shredded mozzarella cheese
- 1/2 cup marinated artichoke hearts, drained and chopped
- 1/4 cup sun-dried tomatoes, drained and chopped
- 2 cloves garlic, minced
- 2 tablespoons extra-virgin olive oil
- Salt and pepper to taste
- Crushed red pepper flakes (optional)
- Fresh basil leaves (optional)
- Cornmeal or flour for dusting

Instructions:

1. Preheat your oven to the highest temperature it can go, typically around 500-550°F (260-290°C). If you have a pizza stone, place it in the oven to preheat as well.
2. In a small skillet, heat the extra-virgin olive oil over medium heat. Add the minced garlic and cook for 1-2 minutes until fragrant. Remove from heat and set aside.
3. Dust your work surface with cornmeal or flour to prevent sticking. Stretch or roll out the pizza dough into a circle, about 12 inches in diameter, or your desired thickness.
4. Transfer the stretched dough to a pizza peel or parchment paper dusted with cornmeal or flour.
5. Brush the garlic-infused olive oil evenly over the surface of the pizza dough.
6. Spread the pizza sauce evenly over the dough, leaving a small border around the edges.
7. Sprinkle the shredded mozzarella cheese evenly over the sauce.
8. Distribute the chopped artichoke hearts and sun-dried tomatoes evenly over the cheese.
9. Season with salt and pepper to taste.
10. Optionally, sprinkle crushed red pepper flakes over the pizza for some heat.
11. Carefully transfer the pizza to the preheated oven, either directly onto the pizza stone or onto a baking sheet if you're using parchment paper.

12. Bake the pizza for about 10-12 minutes, or until the crust is golden brown and the cheese is bubbly and melted.
13. Once done, remove the pizza from the oven and let it cool for a minute or two.
14. Optionally, garnish with fresh basil leaves before serving.
15. Slice the Artichoke and Sun-Dried Tomato Pizza and serve hot.

Enjoy the delicious and flavorful combination of ingredients in this pizza!

Caprese Pizza

Ingredients:

- 1 pizza dough (homemade or store-bought)
- 1/2 cup pizza sauce or marinara sauce
- 2 large tomatoes, thinly sliced
- 8 oz fresh mozzarella cheese, sliced
- Fresh basil leaves
- Balsamic glaze (optional)
- Extra-virgin olive oil
- Salt and pepper to taste
- Cornmeal or flour for dusting

Instructions:

1. Preheat your oven to the highest temperature it can go, typically around 500-550°F (260-290°C). If you have a pizza stone, place it in the oven to preheat as well.
2. Dust your work surface with cornmeal or flour to prevent sticking. Stretch or roll out the pizza dough into a circle, about 12 inches in diameter, or your desired thickness.
3. Transfer the stretched dough to a pizza peel or parchment paper dusted with cornmeal or flour.
4. Brush the surface of the dough with a little extra-virgin olive oil.
5. Spread the pizza sauce evenly over the dough, leaving a small border around the edges.
6. Arrange the thinly sliced tomatoes evenly over the sauce.
7. Place the sliced fresh mozzarella cheese over the tomatoes.
8. Tear fresh basil leaves and scatter them over the pizza.
9. Season with salt and pepper to taste.
10. Carefully transfer the pizza to the preheated oven, either directly onto the pizza stone or onto a baking sheet if you're using parchment paper.
11. Bake the pizza for about 10-12 minutes, or until the crust is golden brown and the cheese is bubbly and melted.
12. Once done, remove the pizza from the oven and let it cool for a minute or two.
13. Optionally, drizzle balsamic glaze over the pizza before serving.
14. Slice the Caprese Pizza and serve hot.

Enjoy the fresh and delicious flavors of this classic Italian pizza!

Rustic Meatball Pizza

Ingredients:

For the Meatballs:

- 1/2 pound ground beef
- 1/2 pound ground pork
- 1/4 cup breadcrumbs
- 1/4 cup grated Parmesan cheese
- 1 egg
- 2 cloves garlic, minced
- 1 tablespoon chopped fresh parsley
- Salt and pepper to taste

For the Pizza:

- 1 pizza dough (homemade or store-bought)
- 1/2 cup pizza sauce or marinara sauce
- 1 1/2 cups shredded mozzarella cheese
- 1/4 cup grated Parmesan cheese
- Meatballs (previously prepared)
- Fresh basil leaves, torn (for garnish)
- Olive oil for drizzling
- Cornmeal or flour for dusting

Instructions:

Making the Meatballs:

1. Preheat your oven to 400°F (200°C).
2. In a mixing bowl, combine the ground beef, ground pork, breadcrumbs, grated Parmesan cheese, egg, minced garlic, chopped parsley, salt, and pepper. Mix until well combined.
3. Form the mixture into meatballs, about 1-inch in diameter.
4. Place the meatballs on a baking sheet lined with parchment paper.
5. Bake in the preheated oven for 15-20 minutes, or until the meatballs are cooked through and browned on the outside.
6. Remove from the oven and set aside.

Making the Pizza:

1. Preheat your oven to the highest temperature it can go, typically around 500-550°F (260-290°C). If you have a pizza stone, place it in the oven to preheat as well.
2. Dust your work surface with cornmeal or flour to prevent sticking. Stretch or roll out the pizza dough into a circle, about 12 inches in diameter, or your desired thickness.
3. Transfer the stretched dough to a pizza peel or parchment paper dusted with cornmeal or flour.
4. Drizzle a little olive oil over the dough and spread it evenly with your hands.
5. Spread the pizza sauce evenly over the dough, leaving a small border around the edges.
6. Sprinkle the shredded mozzarella cheese evenly over the sauce.
7. Arrange the cooked meatballs evenly over the cheese.
8. Sprinkle the grated Parmesan cheese over the pizza.
9. Carefully transfer the pizza to the preheated oven, either directly onto the pizza stone or onto a baking sheet if you're using parchment paper.
10. Bake the pizza for about 10-12 minutes, or until the crust is golden brown and the cheese is bubbly and melted.
11. Once done, remove the pizza from the oven and let it cool for a minute or two.
12. Garnish with torn fresh basil leaves before serving.
13. Slice the Rustic Meatball Pizza and serve hot.

Enjoy the comforting flavors of this hearty pizza!

Three Mushroom Pizza

Ingredients:

- 1 pizza dough (homemade or store-bought)
- 1/2 cup pizza sauce or marinara sauce
- 1 1/2 cups shredded mozzarella cheese
- 1 cup mixed mushrooms (such as cremini, shiitake, and oyster), thinly sliced
- 2 cloves garlic, minced
- 2 tablespoons olive oil
- Salt and pepper to taste
- Fresh thyme leaves (optional, for garnish)
- Grated Parmesan cheese (optional)
- Cornmeal or flour for dusting

Instructions:

1. Preheat your oven to the highest temperature it can go, typically around 500-550°F (260-290°C). If you have a pizza stone, place it in the oven to preheat as well.
2. In a skillet, heat the olive oil over medium heat. Add the minced garlic and cook for 1-2 minutes until fragrant. Add the sliced mushrooms to the skillet and cook until they are soft and golden brown, about 5-7 minutes. Season with salt and pepper to taste. Remove from heat and set aside.
3. Dust your work surface with cornmeal or flour to prevent sticking. Stretch or roll out the pizza dough into a circle, about 12 inches in diameter, or your desired thickness.
4. Transfer the stretched dough to a pizza peel or parchment paper dusted with cornmeal or flour.
5. Spread the pizza sauce evenly over the dough, leaving a small border around the edges.
6. Sprinkle the shredded mozzarella cheese evenly over the sauce.
7. Arrange the cooked mushrooms evenly over the cheese.
8. Season with a pinch of salt and pepper to taste.
9. Carefully transfer the pizza to the preheated oven, either directly onto the pizza stone or onto a baking sheet if you're using parchment paper.
10. Bake the pizza for about 10-12 minutes, or until the crust is golden brown and the cheese is bubbly and melted.
11. Once done, remove the pizza from the oven and let it cool for a minute or two.

12. Optionally, garnish with fresh thyme leaves and grated Parmesan cheese before serving.
13. Slice the Three Mushroom Pizza and serve hot.

Enjoy the rich and earthy flavors of this delicious pizza!

Shrimp Scampi Pizza

Ingredients:

- 1 pizza dough (homemade or store-bought)
- 1/2 cup Alfredo sauce
- 1 1/2 cups shredded mozzarella cheese
- 1/2 pound shrimp, peeled and deveined
- 2 cloves garlic, minced
- 2 tablespoons butter
- 2 tablespoons lemon juice
- 2 tablespoons chopped fresh parsley
- Salt and pepper to taste
- Red pepper flakes (optional)
- Olive oil for drizzling
- Cornmeal or flour for dusting

Instructions:

1. Preheat your oven to the highest temperature it can go, typically around 500-550°F (260-290°C). If you have a pizza stone, place it in the oven to preheat as well.
2. In a skillet, melt the butter over medium heat. Add the minced garlic and cook for 1-2 minutes until fragrant.
3. Add the shrimp to the skillet and cook until they turn pink and are cooked through, about 2-3 minutes per side.
4. Stir in the lemon juice and chopped parsley. Season with salt and pepper to taste. Remove from heat and set aside.
5. Dust your work surface with cornmeal or flour to prevent sticking. Stretch or roll out the pizza dough into a circle, about 12 inches in diameter, or your desired thickness.
6. Transfer the stretched dough to a pizza peel or parchment paper dusted with cornmeal or flour.
7. Spread the Alfredo sauce evenly over the dough, leaving a small border around the edges.
8. Sprinkle the shredded mozzarella cheese evenly over the sauce.
9. Arrange the cooked shrimp evenly over the cheese.
10. Optionally, sprinkle red pepper flakes over the pizza for some heat.
11. Drizzle a little olive oil over the pizza.

12. Carefully transfer the pizza to the preheated oven, either directly onto the pizza stone or onto a baking sheet if you're using parchment paper.
13. Bake the pizza for about 10-12 minutes, or until the crust is golden brown and the cheese is bubbly and melted.
14. Once done, remove the pizza from the oven and let it cool for a minute or two.
15. Slice the Shrimp Scampi Pizza and serve hot.

Enjoy the delicious combination of shrimp scampi flavors on a pizza!

Margherita with Burrata

Ingredients:

- 1 pizza dough (homemade or store-bought)
- 1/2 cup pizza sauce or marinara sauce
- 1 1/2 cups shredded mozzarella cheese
- 2 ripe tomatoes, thinly sliced
- 1 ball of burrata cheese
- Fresh basil leaves
- Extra-virgin olive oil
- Salt and pepper to taste
- Cornmeal or flour for dusting

Instructions:

1. Preheat your oven to the highest temperature it can go, typically around 500-550°F (260-290°C). If you have a pizza stone, place it in the oven to preheat as well.
2. Dust your work surface with cornmeal or flour to prevent sticking. Stretch or roll out the pizza dough into a circle, about 12 inches in diameter, or your desired thickness.
3. Transfer the stretched dough to a pizza peel or parchment paper dusted with cornmeal or flour.
4. Brush the surface of the dough with a little extra-virgin olive oil.
5. Spread the pizza sauce evenly over the dough, leaving a small border around the edges.
6. Sprinkle the shredded mozzarella cheese evenly over the sauce.
7. Arrange the thinly sliced tomatoes over the cheese.
8. Tear fresh basil leaves and scatter them over the pizza.
9. Season with salt and pepper to taste.
10. Carefully transfer the pizza to the preheated oven, either directly onto the pizza stone or onto a baking sheet if you're using parchment paper.
11. Bake the pizza for about 10-12 minutes, or until the crust is golden brown and the cheese is bubbly and melted.
12. Once done, remove the pizza from the oven and let it cool for a minute or two.
13. Tear the burrata cheese into pieces and arrange them on top of the pizza.
14. Drizzle a little extra-virgin olive oil over the burrata cheese.
15. Slice the Margherita Pizza with Burrata and serve hot.

Enjoy the creamy and indulgent flavors of this delicious pizza!

Truffle Oil and Mushroom Pizza

Ingredients:

- 1 pizza dough (homemade or store-bought)
- 1/2 cup pizza sauce or marinara sauce
- 1 1/2 cups shredded mozzarella cheese
- 2 cups assorted mushrooms (such as cremini, shiitake, and oyster), thinly sliced
- 2 cloves garlic, minced
- 2 tablespoons truffle oil
- Salt and pepper to taste
- Fresh thyme leaves (optional, for garnish)
- Grated Parmesan cheese (optional)
- Cornmeal or flour for dusting

Instructions:

1. Preheat your oven to the highest temperature it can go, typically around 500-550°F (260-290°C). If you have a pizza stone, place it in the oven to preheat as well.
2. In a skillet, heat a drizzle of olive oil over medium heat. Add the minced garlic and cook for 1-2 minutes until fragrant.
3. Add the sliced mushrooms to the skillet and cook until they are soft and golden brown, about 5-7 minutes. Season with salt and pepper to taste. Remove from heat and set aside.
4. Dust your work surface with cornmeal or flour to prevent sticking. Stretch or roll out the pizza dough into a circle, about 12 inches in diameter, or your desired thickness.
5. Transfer the stretched dough to a pizza peel or parchment paper dusted with cornmeal or flour.
6. Spread the pizza sauce evenly over the dough, leaving a small border around the edges.
7. Sprinkle the shredded mozzarella cheese evenly over the sauce.
8. Arrange the cooked mushrooms evenly over the cheese.
9. Drizzle the truffle oil over the pizza.
10. Carefully transfer the pizza to the preheated oven, either directly onto the pizza stone or onto a baking sheet if you're using parchment paper.
11. Bake the pizza for about 10-12 minutes, or until the crust is golden brown and the cheese is bubbly and melted.

12. Once done, remove the pizza from the oven and let it cool for a minute or two.
13. Optionally, garnish with fresh thyme leaves and grated Parmesan cheese before serving.
14. Slice the Truffle Oil and Mushroom Pizza and serve hot.

Enjoy the luxurious flavors of this gourmet pizza!

Potato and Rosemary Pizza

Ingredients:

- 1 pizza dough (homemade or store-bought)
- 2 medium potatoes, thinly sliced
- 2 tablespoons olive oil
- 2 cloves garlic, minced
- 1 tablespoon fresh rosemary, chopped
- Salt and pepper to taste
- 1 1/2 cups shredded mozzarella cheese
- Grated Parmesan cheese (optional)
- Cornmeal or flour for dusting

Instructions:

1. Preheat your oven to the highest temperature it can go, typically around 500-550°F (260-290°C). If you have a pizza stone, place it in the oven to preheat as well.
2. In a skillet, heat 1 tablespoon of olive oil over medium heat. Add the minced garlic and cook for 1-2 minutes until fragrant.
3. Add the thinly sliced potatoes to the skillet and cook until they are tender and lightly golden brown, about 5-7 minutes. Season with salt and pepper to taste. Remove from heat and set aside.
4. Dust your work surface with cornmeal or flour to prevent sticking. Stretch or roll out the pizza dough into a circle, about 12 inches in diameter, or your desired thickness.
5. Transfer the stretched dough to a pizza peel or parchment paper dusted with cornmeal or flour.
6. Brush the surface of the dough with the remaining tablespoon of olive oil.
7. Sprinkle the chopped rosemary evenly over the dough.
8. Arrange the cooked potato slices evenly over the dough, slightly overlapping them.
9. Sprinkle the shredded mozzarella cheese evenly over the potato slices.
10. Optionally, sprinkle grated Parmesan cheese over the pizza for extra flavor.
11. Carefully transfer the pizza to the preheated oven, either directly onto the pizza stone or onto a baking sheet if you're using parchment paper.
12. Bake the pizza for about 10-12 minutes, or until the crust is golden brown and the cheese is bubbly and melted.

13. Once done, remove the pizza from the oven and let it cool for a minute or two.
14. Slice the Potato and Rosemary Pizza and serve hot.

Enjoy the delicious combination of flavors in this unique pizza!

Margherita with Anchovies

Ingredients:

- 1 pizza dough (homemade or store-bought)
- 1/2 cup pizza sauce or marinara sauce
- 1 1/2 cups shredded mozzarella cheese
- 4-6 anchovy fillets, drained
- Fresh basil leaves
- Extra-virgin olive oil
- Salt and pepper to taste
- Cornmeal or flour for dusting

Instructions:

1. Preheat your oven to the highest temperature it can go, typically around 500-550°F (260-290°C). If you have a pizza stone, place it in the oven to preheat as well.
2. Dust your work surface with cornmeal or flour to prevent sticking. Stretch or roll out the pizza dough into a circle, about 12 inches in diameter, or your desired thickness.
3. Transfer the stretched dough to a pizza peel or parchment paper dusted with cornmeal or flour.
4. Spread the pizza sauce evenly over the dough, leaving a small border around the edges.
5. Sprinkle the shredded mozzarella cheese evenly over the sauce.
6. Arrange the anchovy fillets evenly over the cheese.
7. Tear fresh basil leaves and scatter them over the pizza.
8. Drizzle a little extra-virgin olive oil over the pizza.
9. Season with salt and pepper to taste.
10. Carefully transfer the pizza to the preheated oven, either directly onto the pizza stone or onto a baking sheet if you're using parchment paper.
11. Bake the pizza for about 10-12 minutes, or until the crust is golden brown and the cheese is bubbly and melted.
12. Once done, remove the pizza from the oven and let it cool for a minute or two.
13. Slice the Margherita Pizza with Anchovies and serve hot.

Enjoy the briny and savory flavors of this unique pizza!

Rustic Margherita with Burrata

Ingredients:

- 1 pizza dough (homemade or store-bought)
- 1/2 cup pizza sauce or marinara sauce
- 1 1/2 cups shredded mozzarella cheese
- 2 ripe tomatoes, thinly sliced
- 1 ball of burrata cheese
- Fresh basil leaves
- Extra-virgin olive oil
- Salt and pepper to taste
- Cornmeal or flour for dusting

Instructions:

1. Preheat your oven to the highest temperature it can go, typically around 500-550°F (260-290°C). If you have a pizza stone, place it in the oven to preheat as well.
2. Dust your work surface with cornmeal or flour to prevent sticking. Stretch or roll out the pizza dough into a circle, about 12 inches in diameter, or your desired thickness.
3. Transfer the stretched dough to a pizza peel or parchment paper dusted with cornmeal or flour.
4. Spread the pizza sauce evenly over the dough, leaving a small border around the edges.
5. Sprinkle the shredded mozzarella cheese evenly over the sauce.
6. Arrange the thinly sliced tomatoes over the cheese.
7. Tear fresh basil leaves and scatter them over the pizza.
8. Season with salt and pepper to taste.
9. Drizzle a little extra-virgin olive oil over the pizza.
10. Carefully transfer the pizza to the preheated oven, either directly onto the pizza stone or onto a baking sheet if you're using parchment paper.
11. Bake the pizza for about 10-12 minutes, or until the crust is golden brown and the cheese is bubbly and melted.
12. Once done, remove the pizza from the oven and let it cool for a minute or two.
13. Tear the burrata cheese into pieces and arrange them on top of the pizza.
14. Drizzle a little extra-virgin olive oil over the burrata cheese.
15. Slice the Rustic Margherita Pizza with Burrata and serve hot.

Enjoy the creamy and indulgent flavors of this delicious pizza!

Margherita with Prosciutto Crudo

Ingredients:

- 1 pizza dough (homemade or store-bought)
- 1/2 cup pizza sauce or marinara sauce
- 1 1/2 cups shredded mozzarella cheese
- 4-6 slices of prosciutto crudo
- Fresh basil leaves
- Extra-virgin olive oil
- Salt and pepper to taste
- Cornmeal or flour for dusting

Instructions:

1. Preheat your oven to the highest temperature it can go, typically around 500-550°F (260-290°C). If you have a pizza stone, place it in the oven to preheat as well.
2. Dust your work surface with cornmeal or flour to prevent sticking. Stretch or roll out the pizza dough into a circle, about 12 inches in diameter, or your desired thickness.
3. Transfer the stretched dough to a pizza peel or parchment paper dusted with cornmeal or flour.
4. Spread the pizza sauce evenly over the dough, leaving a small border around the edges.
5. Sprinkle the shredded mozzarella cheese evenly over the sauce.
6. Tear fresh basil leaves and scatter them over the pizza.
7. Arrange the slices of prosciutto crudo evenly over the pizza.
8. Drizzle a little extra-virgin olive oil over the pizza.
9. Season with salt and pepper to taste.
10. Carefully transfer the pizza to the preheated oven, either directly onto the pizza stone or onto a baking sheet if you're using parchment paper.
11. Bake the pizza for about 10-12 minutes, or until the crust is golden brown and the cheese is bubbly and melted.
12. Once done, remove the pizza from the oven and let it cool for a minute or two.
13. Slice the Margherita Pizza with Prosciutto Crudo and serve hot.

Enjoy the savory and luxurious flavors of this delicious pizza!

Rustic Veggie Pizza

Ingredients:

- 1 pizza dough (homemade or store-bought)
- 1/2 cup pizza sauce or marinara sauce
- 1 1/2 cups shredded mozzarella cheese
- Assorted vegetables (such as bell peppers, red onions, cherry tomatoes, zucchini, mushrooms, and olives), thinly sliced or chopped
- 2 cloves garlic, minced
- 2 tablespoons olive oil
- Salt and pepper to taste
- Fresh basil leaves (optional, for garnish)
- Grated Parmesan cheese (optional)
- Cornmeal or flour for dusting

Instructions:

1. Preheat your oven to the highest temperature it can go, typically around 500-550°F (260-290°C). If you have a pizza stone, place it in the oven to preheat as well.
2. In a skillet, heat the olive oil over medium heat. Add the minced garlic and cook for 1-2 minutes until fragrant.
3. Add the assorted vegetables to the skillet and cook until they are tender and slightly caramelized, about 5-7 minutes. Season with salt and pepper to taste. Remove from heat and set aside.
4. Dust your work surface with cornmeal or flour to prevent sticking. Stretch or roll out the pizza dough into a circle, about 12 inches in diameter, or your desired thickness.
5. Transfer the stretched dough to a pizza peel or parchment paper dusted with cornmeal or flour.
6. Spread the pizza sauce evenly over the dough, leaving a small border around the edges.
7. Sprinkle the shredded mozzarella cheese evenly over the sauce.
8. Arrange the cooked vegetables evenly over the cheese.
9. Season with salt and pepper to taste.
10. Carefully transfer the pizza to the preheated oven, either directly onto the pizza stone or onto a baking sheet if you're using parchment paper.

11. Bake the pizza for about 10-12 minutes, or until the crust is golden brown and the cheese is bubbly and melted.
12. Once done, remove the pizza from the oven and let it cool for a minute or two.
13. Optionally, garnish with fresh basil leaves and grated Parmesan cheese before serving.
14. Slice the Rustic Veggie Pizza and serve hot.

Enjoy the fresh and vibrant flavors of this delicious pizza!

Margherita with Fresh Mozzarella

Ingredients:

- 1 pizza dough (homemade or store-bought)
- 1/2 cup pizza sauce or marinara sauce
- 8 oz fresh mozzarella cheese, thinly sliced
- 2 ripe tomatoes, thinly sliced
- Fresh basil leaves
- Extra-virgin olive oil
- Salt and pepper to taste
- Cornmeal or flour for dusting

Instructions:

1. Preheat your oven to the highest temperature it can go, typically around 500-550°F (260-290°C). If you have a pizza stone, place it in the oven to preheat as well.
2. Dust your work surface with cornmeal or flour to prevent sticking. Stretch or roll out the pizza dough into a circle, about 12 inches in diameter, or your desired thickness.
3. Transfer the stretched dough to a pizza peel or parchment paper dusted with cornmeal or flour.
4. Brush the surface of the dough with a little extra-virgin olive oil.
5. Spread the pizza sauce evenly over the dough, leaving a small border around the edges.
6. Arrange the thinly sliced fresh mozzarella cheese over the sauce.
7. Place the thinly sliced tomatoes over the mozzarella cheese.
8. Tear fresh basil leaves and scatter them over the pizza.
9. Season with salt and pepper to taste.
10. Drizzle a little extra-virgin olive oil over the pizza.
11. Carefully transfer the pizza to the preheated oven, either directly onto the pizza stone or onto a baking sheet if you're using parchment paper.
12. Bake the pizza for about 10-12 minutes, or until the crust is golden brown and the cheese is bubbly and melted.
13. Once done, remove the pizza from the oven and let it cool for a minute or two.
14. Slice the Margherita Pizza with Fresh Mozzarella and serve hot.

Enjoy the fresh and delicious flavors of this classic pizza!

Rustic Italian Sausage and Peppers Pizza

Ingredients:

- 1 pizza dough (homemade or store-bought)
- 1/2 cup pizza sauce or marinara sauce
- 1 1/2 cups shredded mozzarella cheese
- 1/2 pound Italian sausage, cooked and crumbled
- 1 bell pepper (any color), thinly sliced
- 1/2 onion, thinly sliced
- 2 cloves garlic, minced
- 1 tablespoon olive oil
- Salt and pepper to taste
- Crushed red pepper flakes (optional)
- Fresh basil leaves (optional, for garnish)
- Grated Parmesan cheese (optional)
- Cornmeal or flour for dusting

Instructions:

1. Preheat your oven to the highest temperature it can go, typically around 500-550°F (260-290°C). If you have a pizza stone, place it in the oven to preheat as well.
2. In a skillet, heat the olive oil over medium heat. Add the minced garlic and cook for 1-2 minutes until fragrant.
3. Add the thinly sliced bell pepper and onion to the skillet. Cook until they are softened and slightly caramelized, about 5-7 minutes. Season with salt and pepper to taste. Remove from heat and set aside.
4. Dust your work surface with cornmeal or flour to prevent sticking. Stretch or roll out the pizza dough into a circle, about 12 inches in diameter, or your desired thickness.
5. Transfer the stretched dough to a pizza peel or parchment paper dusted with cornmeal or flour.
6. Spread the pizza sauce evenly over the dough, leaving a small border around the edges.
7. Sprinkle the shredded mozzarella cheese evenly over the sauce.
8. Scatter the cooked Italian sausage crumbles over the cheese.
9. Arrange the cooked bell peppers and onions evenly over the pizza.
10. Optionally, sprinkle crushed red pepper flakes over the pizza for some heat.

11. Carefully transfer the pizza to the preheated oven, either directly onto the pizza stone or onto a baking sheet if you're using parchment paper.
12. Bake the pizza for about 10-12 minutes, or until the crust is golden brown and the cheese is bubbly and melted.
13. Once done, remove the pizza from the oven and let it cool for a minute or two.
14. Optionally, garnish with fresh basil leaves and grated Parmesan cheese before serving.
15. Slice the Rustic Italian Sausage and Peppers Pizza and serve hot.

Enjoy the delicious combination of flavors in this hearty pizza!

Margherita with Ricotta Cheese

Ingredients:

- 1 pizza dough (homemade or store-bought)
- 1/2 cup pizza sauce or marinara sauce
- 1 1/2 cups shredded mozzarella cheese
- 1/2 cup ricotta cheese
- 2 ripe tomatoes, thinly sliced
- Fresh basil leaves
- Extra-virgin olive oil
- Salt and pepper to taste
- Cornmeal or flour for dusting

Instructions:

1. Preheat your oven to the highest temperature it can go, typically around 500-550°F (260-290°C). If you have a pizza stone, place it in the oven to preheat as well.
2. Dust your work surface with cornmeal or flour to prevent sticking. Stretch or roll out the pizza dough into a circle, about 12 inches in diameter, or your desired thickness.
3. Transfer the stretched dough to a pizza peel or parchment paper dusted with cornmeal or flour.
4. Spread the pizza sauce evenly over the dough, leaving a small border around the edges.
5. Sprinkle the shredded mozzarella cheese evenly over the sauce.
6. Spoon dollops of ricotta cheese evenly over the pizza.
7. Place the thinly sliced tomatoes over the cheese and ricotta.
8. Tear fresh basil leaves and scatter them over the pizza.
9. Drizzle a little extra-virgin olive oil over the pizza.
10. Season with salt and pepper to taste.
11. Carefully transfer the pizza to the preheated oven, either directly onto the pizza stone or onto a baking sheet if you're using parchment paper.
12. Bake the pizza for about 10-12 minutes, or until the crust is golden brown and the cheese is bubbly and melted.
13. Once done, remove the pizza from the oven and let it cool for a minute or two.
14. Slice the Margherita Pizza with Ricotta Cheese and serve hot.

Enjoy the creamy and delicious flavors of this Margherita variation!

Rustic Italian Meat Lovers Pizza

Ingredients:

- 1 pizza dough (homemade or store-bought)
- 1/2 cup pizza sauce or marinara sauce
- 1 1/2 cups shredded mozzarella cheese
- 1/4 pound Italian sausage, cooked and crumbled
- 1/4 pound pepperoni slices
- 1/4 pound cooked bacon, chopped
- 1/4 pound cooked ham, diced
- 2 cloves garlic, minced
- 1 tablespoon olive oil
- Salt and pepper to taste
- Crushed red pepper flakes (optional)
- Fresh basil leaves (optional, for garnish)
- Grated Parmesan cheese (optional)
- Cornmeal or flour for dusting

Instructions:

1. Preheat your oven to the highest temperature it can go, typically around 500-550°F (260-290°C). If you have a pizza stone, place it in the oven to preheat as well.
2. In a skillet, heat the olive oil over medium heat. Add the minced garlic and cook for 1-2 minutes until fragrant.
3. Add the cooked Italian sausage, pepperoni slices, chopped bacon, and diced ham to the skillet. Cook for another 2-3 minutes to heat through.
4. Dust your work surface with cornmeal or flour to prevent sticking. Stretch or roll out the pizza dough into a circle, about 12 inches in diameter, or your desired thickness.
5. Transfer the stretched dough to a pizza peel or parchment paper dusted with cornmeal or flour.
6. Spread the pizza sauce evenly over the dough, leaving a small border around the edges.
7. Sprinkle the shredded mozzarella cheese evenly over the sauce.
8. Scatter the cooked meat mixture evenly over the cheese.
9. Optionally, sprinkle crushed red pepper flakes over the pizza for some heat.

10. Carefully transfer the pizza to the preheated oven, either directly onto the pizza stone or onto a baking sheet if you're using parchment paper.
11. Bake the pizza for about 10-12 minutes, or until the crust is golden brown and the cheese is bubbly and melted.
12. Once done, remove the pizza from the oven and let it cool for a minute or two.
13. Optionally, garnish with fresh basil leaves and grated Parmesan cheese before serving.
14. Slice the Rustic Italian Meat Lovers Pizza and serve hot.

Enjoy the savory and delicious flavors of this hearty pizza!

Margherita with Spinach and Ricotta

Ingredients:

- 1 pizza dough (homemade or store-bought)
- 1/2 cup pizza sauce or marinara sauce
- 1 1/2 cups shredded mozzarella cheese
- 1/2 cup ricotta cheese
- 1 cup fresh spinach leaves, washed and dried
- 2 cloves garlic, minced
- 1 tablespoon olive oil
- Salt and pepper to taste
- Crushed red pepper flakes (optional)
- Fresh basil leaves (optional, for garnish)
- Grated Parmesan cheese (optional)
- Cornmeal or flour for dusting

Instructions:

1. Preheat your oven to the highest temperature it can go, typically around 500-550°F (260-290°C). If you have a pizza stone, place it in the oven to preheat as well.
2. In a skillet, heat the olive oil over medium heat. Add the minced garlic and cook for 1-2 minutes until fragrant.
3. Add the fresh spinach leaves to the skillet and cook until wilted, about 2-3 minutes. Season with salt and pepper to taste. Remove from heat and set aside.
4. Dust your work surface with cornmeal or flour to prevent sticking. Stretch or roll out the pizza dough into a circle, about 12 inches in diameter, or your desired thickness.
5. Transfer the stretched dough to a pizza peel or parchment paper dusted with cornmeal or flour.
6. Spread the pizza sauce evenly over the dough, leaving a small border around the edges.
7. Sprinkle the shredded mozzarella cheese evenly over the sauce.
8. Spoon dollops of ricotta cheese evenly over the pizza.
9. Arrange the cooked spinach evenly over the cheese.
10. Optionally, sprinkle crushed red pepper flakes over the pizza for some heat.
11. Carefully transfer the pizza to the preheated oven, either directly onto the pizza stone or onto a baking sheet if you're using parchment paper.

12. Bake the pizza for about 10-12 minutes, or until the crust is golden brown and the cheese is bubbly and melted.
13. Once done, remove the pizza from the oven and let it cool for a minute or two.
14. Optionally, garnish with fresh basil leaves and grated Parmesan cheese before serving.
15. Slice the Margherita Pizza with Spinach and Ricotta and serve hot.

Enjoy the delicious and nutritious flavors of this unique pizza!

Rustic Margherita with Fresh Tomatoes

Ingredients:

- 1 pizza dough (homemade or store-bought)
- 1/2 cup pizza sauce or marinara sauce
- 1 1/2 cups shredded mozzarella cheese
- 1/2 cup ricotta cheese
- 1 cup fresh spinach leaves, washed and dried
- 2 cloves garlic, minced
- 1 tablespoon olive oil
- Salt and pepper to taste
- Crushed red pepper flakes (optional)
- Fresh basil leaves (optional, for garnish)
- Grated Parmesan cheese (optional)
- Cornmeal or flour for dusting

Instructions:

1. Preheat your oven to the highest temperature it can go, typically around 500-550°F (260-290°C). If you have a pizza stone, place it in the oven to preheat as well.
2. In a skillet, heat the olive oil over medium heat. Add the minced garlic and cook for 1-2 minutes until fragrant.
3. Add the fresh spinach leaves to the skillet and cook until wilted, about 2-3 minutes. Season with salt and pepper to taste. Remove from heat and set aside.
4. Dust your work surface with cornmeal or flour to prevent sticking. Stretch or roll out the pizza dough into a circle, about 12 inches in diameter, or your desired thickness.
5. Transfer the stretched dough to a pizza peel or parchment paper dusted with cornmeal or flour.
6. Spread the pizza sauce evenly over the dough, leaving a small border around the edges.
7. Sprinkle the shredded mozzarella cheese evenly over the sauce.
8. Spoon dollops of ricotta cheese evenly over the pizza.
9. Arrange the cooked spinach evenly over the cheese.
10. Optionally, sprinkle crushed red pepper flakes over the pizza for some heat.
11. Carefully transfer the pizza to the preheated oven, either directly onto the pizza stone or onto a baking sheet if you're using parchment paper.

12. Bake the pizza for about 10-12 minutes, or until the crust is golden brown and the cheese is bubbly and melted.
13. Once done, remove the pizza from the oven and let it cool for a minute or two.
14. Optionally, garnish with fresh basil leaves and grated Parmesan cheese before serving.
15. Slice the Margherita Pizza with Spinach and Ricotta and serve hot.

Enjoy the delicious and nutritious flavors of this unique pizza!

Rustic Margherita with Fresh Tomatoes

Ingredients:

- 1 pizza dough (homemade or store-bought)
- 1/2 cup pizza sauce or marinara sauce
- 2 ripe tomatoes, thinly sliced
- 1 1/2 cups shredded mozzarella cheese
- Fresh basil leaves
- Extra-virgin olive oil
- Salt and pepper to taste
- Cornmeal or flour for dusting

Instructions:

1. Preheat your oven to the highest temperature it can go, typically around 500-550°F (260-290°C). If you have a pizza stone, place it in the oven to preheat as well.
2. Dust your work surface with cornmeal or flour to prevent sticking. Stretch or roll out the pizza dough into a circle, about 12 inches in diameter, or your desired thickness.
3. Transfer the stretched dough to a pizza peel or parchment paper dusted with cornmeal or flour.
4. Spread the pizza sauce evenly over the dough, leaving a small border around the edges.
5. Arrange the thinly sliced tomatoes over the sauce.
6. Sprinkle the shredded mozzarella cheese evenly over the tomatoes.
7. Tear fresh basil leaves and scatter them over the pizza.
8. Drizzle a little extra-virgin olive oil over the pizza.
9. Season with salt and pepper to taste.
10. Carefully transfer the pizza to the preheated oven, either directly onto the pizza stone or onto a baking sheet if you're using parchment paper.
11. Bake the pizza for about 10-12 minutes, or until the crust is golden brown and the cheese is bubbly and melted.
12. Once done, remove the pizza from the oven and let it cool for a minute or two.
13. Slice the Rustic Margherita Pizza with Fresh Tomatoes and serve hot.

Enjoy the fresh and vibrant flavors of this classic pizza!

Margherita with Italian Ham

Ingredients:

- 1 pizza dough (homemade or store-bought)
- 1/2 cup pizza sauce or marinara sauce
- 1 1/2 cups shredded mozzarella cheese
- 4-6 slices Italian ham (such as prosciutto or speck)
- 2 ripe tomatoes, thinly sliced
- Fresh basil leaves
- Extra-virgin olive oil
- Salt and pepper to taste
- Cornmeal or flour for dusting

Instructions:

1. Preheat your oven to the highest temperature it can go, typically around 500-550°F (260-290°C). If you have a pizza stone, place it in the oven to preheat as well.
2. Dust your work surface with cornmeal or flour to prevent sticking. Stretch or roll out the pizza dough into a circle, about 12 inches in diameter, or your desired thickness.
3. Transfer the stretched dough to a pizza peel or parchment paper dusted with cornmeal or flour.
4. Spread the pizza sauce evenly over the dough, leaving a small border around the edges.
5. Sprinkle the shredded mozzarella cheese evenly over the sauce.
6. Arrange the thinly sliced tomatoes over the cheese.
7. Tear fresh basil leaves and scatter them over the pizza.
8. Place the slices of Italian ham evenly over the pizza.
9. Drizzle a little extra-virgin olive oil over the pizza.
10. Season with salt and pepper to taste.
11. Carefully transfer the pizza to the preheated oven, either directly onto the pizza stone or onto a baking sheet if you're using parchment paper.
12. Bake the pizza for about 10-12 minutes, or until the crust is golden brown and the cheese is bubbly and melted.
13. Once done, remove the pizza from the oven and let it cool for a minute or two.
14. Slice the Margherita Pizza with Italian Ham and serve hot.

Enjoy the savory and delicious flavors of this unique pizza!

Rustic Margherita with Pesto Drizzle

Ingredients:

- 1 pizza dough (homemade or store-bought)
- 1/2 cup pizza sauce or marinara sauce
- 1 1/2 cups shredded mozzarella cheese
- 2 ripe tomatoes, thinly sliced
- Fresh basil leaves
- Pesto sauce
- Extra-virgin olive oil
- Salt and pepper to taste
- Cornmeal or flour for dusting

Instructions:

1. Preheat your oven to the highest temperature it can go, typically around 500-550°F (260-290°C). If you have a pizza stone, place it in the oven to preheat as well.
2. Dust your work surface with cornmeal or flour to prevent sticking. Stretch or roll out the pizza dough into a circle, about 12 inches in diameter, or your desired thickness.
3. Transfer the stretched dough to a pizza peel or parchment paper dusted with cornmeal or flour.
4. Spread the pizza sauce evenly over the dough, leaving a small border around the edges.
5. Arrange the thinly sliced tomatoes over the sauce.
6. Sprinkle the shredded mozzarella cheese evenly over the tomatoes.
7. Tear fresh basil leaves and scatter them over the pizza.
8. Drizzle a little extra-virgin olive oil over the pizza.
9. Season with salt and pepper to taste.
10. Carefully transfer the pizza to the preheated oven, either directly onto the pizza stone or onto a baking sheet if you're using parchment paper.
11. Bake the pizza for about 10-12 minutes, or until the crust is golden brown and the cheese is bubbly and melted.
12. Once done, remove the pizza from the oven and let it cool for a minute or two.
13. Drizzle pesto sauce over the cooked pizza in a zigzag pattern or as desired.
14. Slice the Rustic Margherita Pizza with Pesto Drizzle and serve hot.

Enjoy the fresh and vibrant flavors of this unique pizza!

Margherita with Gorgonzola Cheese

Ingredients:

- 1 pizza dough (homemade or store-bought)
- 1/2 cup pizza sauce or marinara sauce
- 1 1/2 cups shredded mozzarella cheese
- 1/4 cup crumbled Gorgonzola cheese
- 2 ripe tomatoes, thinly sliced
- Fresh basil leaves
- Extra-virgin olive oil
- Salt and pepper to taste
- Cornmeal or flour for dusting

Instructions:

1. Preheat your oven to the highest temperature it can go, typically around 500-550°F (260-290°C). If you have a pizza stone, place it in the oven to preheat as well.
2. Dust your work surface with cornmeal or flour to prevent sticking. Stretch or roll out the pizza dough into a circle, about 12 inches in diameter, or your desired thickness.
3. Transfer the stretched dough to a pizza peel or parchment paper dusted with cornmeal or flour.
4. Spread the pizza sauce evenly over the dough, leaving a small border around the edges.
5. Sprinkle the shredded mozzarella cheese evenly over the sauce.
6. Arrange the thinly sliced tomatoes over the cheese.
7. Sprinkle the crumbled Gorgonzola cheese evenly over the pizza.
8. Tear fresh basil leaves and scatter them over the pizza.
9. Drizzle a little extra-virgin olive oil over the pizza.
10. Season with salt and pepper to taste.
11. Carefully transfer the pizza to the preheated oven, either directly onto the pizza stone or onto a baking sheet if you're using parchment paper.
12. Bake the pizza for about 10-12 minutes, or until the crust is golden brown and the cheese is bubbly and melted.
13. Once done, remove the pizza from the oven and let it cool for a minute or two.
14. Slice the Margherita Pizza with Gorgonzola Cheese and serve hot.

Enjoy the rich and tangy flavors of this delicious pizza!

Rustic Margherita with Arugula

Ingredients:

- 1 pizza dough (homemade or store-bought)
- 1/2 cup pizza sauce or marinara sauce
- 1 1/2 cups shredded mozzarella cheese
- 2 ripe tomatoes, thinly sliced
- Handful of fresh arugula leaves
- Fresh basil leaves
- Extra-virgin olive oil
- Salt and pepper to taste
- Cornmeal or flour for dusting

Instructions:

1. Preheat your oven to the highest temperature it can go, typically around 500-550°F (260-290°C). If you have a pizza stone, place it in the oven to preheat as well.
2. Dust your work surface with cornmeal or flour to prevent sticking. Stretch or roll out the pizza dough into a circle, about 12 inches in diameter, or your desired thickness.
3. Transfer the stretched dough to a pizza peel or parchment paper dusted with cornmeal or flour.
4. Spread the pizza sauce evenly over the dough, leaving a small border around the edges.
5. Arrange the thinly sliced tomatoes over the sauce.
6. Sprinkle the shredded mozzarella cheese evenly over the tomatoes.
7. Tear fresh basil leaves and scatter them over the pizza.
8. Drizzle a little extra-virgin olive oil over the pizza.
9. Season with salt and pepper to taste.
10. Carefully transfer the pizza to the preheated oven, either directly onto the pizza stone or onto a baking sheet if you're using parchment paper.
11. Bake the pizza for about 10-12 minutes, or until the crust is golden brown and the cheese is bubbly and melted.
12. Once done, remove the pizza from the oven and let it cool for a minute or two.
13. Scatter fresh arugula leaves over the hot pizza.
14. Slice the Rustic Margherita Pizza with Arugula and serve hot.

Enjoy the fresh and peppery flavors of this delicious pizza!

Margherita with Provolone Cheese

Ingredients:

- 1 whole wheat pizza crust (store-bought or homemade)
- 1/2 cup tomato sauce (preferably low-sodium)
- 1 cup shredded provolone cheese
- 1 cup fresh mozzarella cheese, sliced
- 2-3 fresh tomatoes, thinly sliced
- Fresh basil leaves
- 1-2 tablespoons extra-virgin olive oil
- Salt and pepper to taste

Instructions:

1. Preheat Oven: Preheat your oven to 450°F (230°C). If you have a pizza stone, place it in the oven while it heats up.
2. Prepare Crust: Roll out your whole wheat pizza crust on a lightly floured surface to your desired thickness. Transfer it to a parchment paper-lined baking sheet or a pizza peel if using a pizza stone.
3. Tomato Sauce: Spread the tomato sauce evenly over the pizza crust, leaving a small border around the edges.
4. Add Cheese: Sprinkle the shredded provolone cheese evenly over the tomato sauce. Arrange the fresh mozzarella slices on top of the provolone.
5. Tomatoes and Basil: Lay the tomato slices evenly over the cheese. Scatter fresh basil leaves over the top.
6. Seasoning: Drizzle the extra-virgin olive oil over the pizza. Season with a pinch of salt and a grind of fresh black pepper.
7. Bake: Carefully transfer the pizza to the preheated oven (or onto the pizza stone). Bake for 10-15 minutes, or until the crust is golden and the cheese is bubbly and slightly browned.
8. Serve: Remove the pizza from the oven. Let it cool for a couple of minutes, then slice and serve.

Enjoy your delicious Margherita pizza with provolone cheese!

Rustic Margherita with Pancetta

Ingredients:

- 1 whole wheat pizza crust (store-bought or homemade)
- 1/2 cup tomato sauce (preferably low-sodium)
- 1 cup shredded provolone cheese
- 1 cup fresh mozzarella cheese, sliced
- 2-3 fresh tomatoes, thinly sliced
- 3-4 oz pancetta, thinly sliced
- Fresh basil leaves
- 1-2 tablespoons extra-virgin olive oil
- Salt and pepper to taste

Instructions:

1. Preheat Oven: Preheat your oven to 450°F (230°C). If you have a pizza stone, place it in the oven while it heats up.
2. Prepare Crust: Roll out your whole wheat pizza crust on a lightly floured surface to your desired thickness. Transfer it to a parchment paper-lined baking sheet or a pizza peel if using a pizza stone.
3. Tomato Sauce: Spread the tomato sauce evenly over the pizza crust, leaving a small border around the edges.
4. Add Cheese: Sprinkle the shredded provolone cheese evenly over the tomato sauce. Arrange the fresh mozzarella slices on top of the provolone.
5. Tomatoes and Pancetta: Lay the tomato slices evenly over the cheese. Scatter the thinly sliced pancetta over the top.
6. Seasoning and Basil: Drizzle the extra-virgin olive oil over the pizza. Season with a pinch of salt and a grind of fresh black pepper. Add fresh basil leaves on top.
7. Bake: Carefully transfer the pizza to the preheated oven (or onto the pizza stone). Bake for 10-15 minutes, or until the crust is golden and the cheese is bubbly and slightly browned, and the pancetta is crispy.
8. Serve: Remove the pizza from the oven. Let it cool for a couple of minutes, then slice and serve.

Enjoy your delicious Rustic Margherita pizza with pancetta!

Margherita with Grilled Vegetables

Ingredients:

- 1 whole wheat pizza crust (store-bought or homemade)
- 1/2 cup tomato sauce (preferably low-sodium)
- 1 cup shredded mozzarella cheese
- 1 cup cherry tomatoes, halved
- 1 small zucchini, thinly sliced lengthwise
- 1 small yellow squash, thinly sliced lengthwise
- 1 small red bell pepper, thinly sliced
- 1 small red onion, thinly sliced
- 2 cloves garlic, minced
- 2 tablespoons extra-virgin olive oil
- Salt and pepper to taste
- Fresh basil leaves, torn, for garnish

Instructions:

1. Preheat Grill: Preheat your grill to medium-high heat.
2. Prepare Vegetables: In a large bowl, toss the zucchini, yellow squash, red bell pepper, red onion, and minced garlic with olive oil, salt, and pepper until evenly coated.
3. Grill Vegetables: Place the vegetables on the preheated grill and cook for 3-4 minutes per side, or until they are tender and have grill marks. Remove from the grill and set aside.
4. Prepare Crust: Roll out your whole wheat pizza crust on a lightly floured surface to your desired thickness. Transfer it to a parchment paper-lined baking sheet.
5. Assemble Pizza: Spread the tomato sauce evenly over the pizza crust, leaving a small border around the edges. Sprinkle the shredded mozzarella cheese over the sauce. Arrange the grilled vegetables and cherry tomato halves on top of the cheese.
6. Bake: Carefully transfer the pizza to the preheated grill or onto a pizza stone in the grill. Close the lid and cook for 8-10 minutes, or until the crust is golden brown and the cheese is melted and bubbly.
7. Serve: Remove the pizza from the grill and let it cool for a few minutes. Garnish with torn fresh basil leaves before slicing and serving.

Enjoy your Margherita pizza with grilled vegetables!